LIGHTING THE WAY
· · · · · · · · · · · · · ·

LIGHTING THE WAY

A 12-SESSION SMALL GROUP EXPLORATION
VIA DIALOG OF PAUL'S LETTER TO THE ROMANS

BASED ON THE BOOK, *THE WAY*, WRITTEN BY
JOHN DANNEMILLER AND IRVING STUBBS

ADAPTED FOR USE BY SMALL GROUPS BY
BRIAN REGRUT

Lighting the Way
© 2021 Living Dialog Ministries
PO Box 15125
Richmond, VA 23227

All Rights Reserved

Published in the United States of America by Living Dialog Ministries, a 501(c)(3) tax exempt organization. www.livingdialog.org

ISBN 978-0-9890791-5-0

Scripture quotations, unless otherwise indicated, are taken from the HOLY BIBLE NEW INTERNATIONAL VERSION. Copyright © 1973, 1978, 1984, 2011 by International Bible Society. Used by permission of Zondervan. All rights reserved.

Cover and interior design by Frank Gutbrod

18 17 16 15 14 13 7 6 5 4 3 2 1

Printed in the United States of America

CONTENTS

INTRODUCTION 07

SESSION 1: How did Paul represent himself to the Roman Christians? 13

SESSION 2: What is God's righteous judgement? 19

SESSION 3: What is the way to be right with God? 24

SESSION 4: What comes with Peace with God? 29

SESSION 5: What drives spiritual transformation? 32

SESSION 6: What is the relationship between the Law and Sin? 36

SESSION 7: How do we share in Christ's glory? 41

SESSION 8: Is there hope for the Jews? 46

SESSION 9: What is the message of salvation to all? 50

SESSION 10: What does serious love call for? 54

SESSION 11: How do we live the example of Christ? 60

SESSION 12: How do you close a letter like Paul's to the Romans? 64

EPILOGUE 69

INTRODUCTION

We've designed this 12-session study to help small groups engage in dialog about the Apostle Paul's letter to the followers of Christ who lived in Rome. These believers called themselves "the Way", describing their belief that Jesus was "the way" to God. In his letter, Paul lays down the principal doctrines of Christianity that have guided the Church for two millennia. As we read this letter, we'll encourage exploration of the fundamentals of the Christian life and we'll see how Paul shines a bright light on God's "good news" — "Lighting the Way" for seekers of truth.

Our hope is that as you read the scripture, wrestle with the questions, and listen to what others are discovering, you will gain a richer understanding of the life, teachings, death and resurrection of Jesus and what it means to be transformed into a Child of God. Rich in theology, and essential to evangelism, this study offers a new and refreshing guide to the Apostle Paul's letter to the Romans. If you have questions about what you've heard about Jesus or Christianity or the church, if you have questions you'd like to have asked Paul, you will find these twelve sessions of study stimulating and enlightening.

We'll be getting to know God better by exploring his desire from the beginning of time to be in right relationship with his finest creation—men and women made in his image. We'll see how mankind turned its back on its creator and opened a chasm that had to be bridged through a blood sacrifice. That sacrifice was made by God's son on a Roman cross and was followed by his resurrection. This study will help participants better understand this transaction that provides the means for all who believe to know eternal life with God. Through dialog we'll be learning as we relate to one another during transforming conversations and discussions.

Despite the benefits that many experience through modern communication systems, most of our day-to-day messaging is relatively superficial. Most of the global population is conditioned to skim along the surface of ideas and events without discovering the profound truths that lie deep inside them. This study is designed to buck that trend.

Truthfully, experiences are richer when they're shared. If you experienced a miraculous life event or experience and saw things you'd never seen before, wouldn't you want to tell someone about it? Better yet, wouldn't you like to have someone along to share the "Wow!"?

In your assembly of companions listening anew to a 2000-year-old letter that is as important today as when it was written, you are invited to share your thoughts and experiences through dialog. We believe the meaning of the word "dialog" is a "big" talk, a heart-to-heart sharing that has the power to transform everyone participating in the conversation. Our goal is simple. When you experience this study, our hope and prayer is: You will know Jesus and Christianity as you've never known them before, and that you will become a more confident, bold, courageous and mature believer who "Lights the Way" for others to follow Jesus so that they too can experience God's Grace, Forgiveness, Peace and Love.

Kinds of dialogs

There are different kinds of dialogs we'll experience during our gatherings:

- *Dialog with God* — We believe that God calls each of us to a relationship with him. This relationship gives meaning and purpose to our lives. God wants deep, personal, and open communication with us.

- *Dialog with self* — As you think about what Paul is writing and what it means for the church in the 21st century, you may have thoughts and feelings that clarify, stretch, and challenge your understanding of Jesus and Christianity. You may think, "Is that what Jesus really meant?", "I wonder what Paul is really saying by that?" or "I never thought about it that way before."

- *Dialog with others who are physically present* — The exchange of thoughts and feelings amplify and deepen your understanding. Some of us learn of Jesus, from the word of others.

- *Dialog with others who aren't present* — The words and ideas of others you've known interact with your own thoughts and shape your perceptions in both positive and negative ways.

Invitation to dialog

The kind of dialog we want to cultivate in our group is not another word for "discussion" or "debate". Discussion is analytical and typically picks things apart. In debate, sides work to win points. Dialog, on the other hand, is a way for us together to seek understanding.

Dialog is intended:
- not to advocate but inquire
- not to argue but explore
- not to convince but discover

We listen to one another to find out what is meant. We assume each member of the group has a piece of the answer to the question, and that together, the group can craft a new and better answer. We celebrate new insights, greater clarity, and deeper understandings when they occur.

Agreement is not the purpose of dialog. It is important to suspend judgment about others' contributions. Disagreements can be seen as a different way of looking at a subject. Disagreements can energize a group to seek meaning and clarity that goes beyond initial conflicting views.

How to use this guide

These twelve sessions will guide your group in dialog with Paul and with one another through powerful messages about God, his son, Jesus, the Holy Spirit, the church and what Christianity is all about.

This guide couldn't be simpler to use. No advance preparation or study is required! Some groups may choose to begin each gathering with prayer, or take a few minutes to catch up on one another's lives.

To initiate your time of dialog, your facilitator or someone from your group will read a few brief paragraphs that are a mix of summary and direct quotations from the Bible. Immediately following each section, you'll find a question or two designed to launch your group into dialog over the ideas and issues raised in the text. Your group should stop at the end of each segment to consider the questions that are posed before moving onto the next segment of text. The questions will look like this:

> Are you open to experiencing a spiritual transformation? Why or why not?

You'll find additional questions at the end of each session if your group is looking for further discussion for personal reflection.

Plan on an hour or so for dialog for each meeting. Some groups have gone far beyond an hour due to the intensity and enjoyment of the dialog. Your group's facilitator should be sensitive to the time commitment each member has made to the group. Make sure those in the group agree to go beyond the stated time if extended discussion time seems to be warranted.

Remember that your group's facilitator is there not as an answer man or woman, but as a coach. Each member of your group brings insight and value to the dialog as you craft an answer together. Your facilitator will help to honor your group's time commitment and guide you through the material each week.

You'll close each session with dialog in prayer. Affirming that Christ has been with you as you've shared a meal and talked about his story each week is the foundation for this time. Members of your group may have needs in their lives or questions and concerns raised through the session's dialog. This guide offers some general tips about how to pray conversationally, as well as suggestions for how to shape your prayer experience. Prayer may not be a familiar discipline to you — but it can be as simple as dialoging with a friend. And you are!

Each person must make his or her own decision whether or not to become a follower of Jesus. This decision has eternal implications. We hope and pray that you and your group enjoy your journey with Paul lighting the way. May each member be blessed, challenged, and encouraged as you consider his guidance for becoming a new creation in Christ. Ok, let's get started.

SESSION 1

HOW DID PAUL REPRESENT HIMSELF TO THE ROMAN CHRISTIANS?

Romans 1:1-32

Paul's letter to Christians in Rome is one of the most important descriptions ever written of the Jesus Way. Paul, who once was a zealous persecutor of the people of The Way, was traveling to Damascus to capture Christian heretics when a strange thing happened: He was stopped in his tracks by a dazzling burst of light that seemed greater than the light of the sun. Emerging from the light was the very Jesus whose followers Paul was persecuting. He addressed Paul by his Hebrew name — Saul — and directed him to continue his journey to Damascus where he would be told what he should do. This encounter with the resurrected Jesus changed Paul from a persecutor to the most passionate apostle of early Christendom. In that encounter, Paul became a new creation. He experienced a liberating relationship with God and felt called to proclaim God's gracious offer of reconciliation to the world.

Who was this man Paul? He was from Tarsus, a university city and trade center located in what today is southern Turkey near the Mediterranean coast. That made him a citizen of the Roman Empire. Paul's father must have been well-to-do. He had the means to send his son to school in Jerusalem where his teacher was Gamaliel, an authority on Jewish Law. In addition to his religious training, Paul learned the trade of tent making, probably because Tarsus was a center for the manufacture of a coarse goat hair fabric famous for its durability and used for shoes, mats, and coverings such as tents. This trade ensured that Paul could be self-sufficient wherever he traveled. And travel he did.

His initial opposition to followers of Jesus of Nazareth was primarily in Judea, the territory around Jerusalem in what is now central and southern Israel. But he was soon on his way to Damascus in Syria to arrest Christians and bring them back to Jerusalem for trial as heretics and likely death by stoning. Following his conversion, he continued to Damascus where he was baptized and began proclaiming the good news that Jesus was Christ, the promised messiah. His boldness led to him being threatened by Jewish leaders but with the help of fellow Christians, he escaped the city. (Acts 9)

Paul spent several years in "Arabia" (desert region south and east of Damascus that today includes parts of Syria and Jordan) before returning to Damascus where he again had to flee persecution. During those years in Arabia, Paul says he received instruction via revelation from Jesus himself. (Galations 1:11-18) It was really a "Detox" time and an equiping period to prepare him for his eventual ministry to the Gentiles. Three years after his conversion, Paul returned to Jerusalem where he preached and also entered into disputes with Greek Jews and subsequently headed back to his home town of Tarsus. For the next eight years he remained in what was then known as Asia (today,Turkey) preaching in neighboring towns before being invited to teach in Antioch, the principal seat of Roman governance for Syria and the Eastern Mediterranean region. Finally, 14 years after his conversion, Paul began his missionary travels throughout the Roman empire, preaching, teaching, tent making and planting churches. Another ten years passed before he penned his letter to the church in Rome.

Paul opens his letter with this description of himself:

Paul, a servant of Christ Jesus, called to be an apostle and set apart for the gospel of God — the gospel he promised beforehand through his prophets in the Holy Scriptures regarding his Son, who as to his earthly life was a descendant of David, and who through the Spirit of holiness was appointed the Son of God in power[by his resurrection from the dead: Jesus Christ our Lord. Through him we received grace and apostleship to call all the Gentiles to the obedience that comes from faith for his name's sake. And you also are among those Gentiles who are called to belong to Jesus Christ.

[Romans 1:1-6]

> **What does Paul's introduction tell us about the man and his mission?**

Paul was thankful for the faith of those in Rome — a faith that was reported all over the world. He prayed for them, and now saw the way open to come visit them and give them a spiritual gift to make them strong. Paul was confident that both he and the Christians in Rome would be encouraged by each other's faith. He closed his introduction with these words: "I am not ashamed of the gospel, because it is the power of God for the salvation of everyone who believes: first for the Jew, then for the Gentile." (Romans 1:16) Paul then added that there was no excuse for the behavior of those who live without reference to God the creator since God made it plain enough to live differently. People claimed to be wise, but their behavior proved they were foolish. They had exchanged the glory of the immortal God for the vanity of humans and animals. They had exchanged the truth of God for a lie and worshiped and served created things rather than the Creator.

> - Why do people have a need to worship something or someone?
> - What do you worship? Why?
> - What did Paul mean by "God's invisible qualities have been clearly seen"?

Paul painted a dark picture of the consequences of a "depraved mind": greed, depravity, envy, murder, strife, deceit, malice, gossip, slander, insolence, arrogance, boastfulness, and God-hating. What's more, those who had lost the knowledge of God were also disobedient to parents, senseless, faithless, heartless, and ruthless. Women exchanged natural relations for unnatural ones. Men abandoned natural relations with women and were inflamed with lust for one another. "They exchanged the truth about God for a lie, and worshiped and served created things rather than the Creator—who is forever praised."

[Romans 1:27]

- According to Paul, what is the root cause of the "depraved mind" described in this passage?
- What happens to a society or culture when the consequences of "depraved minds" go unchecked?

Paul expressed grave concerns about the culture that pervaded the Roman Empire, touching on a wide range of behaviors. Later on in his letter he addresses many of these behaviors, but here at the outset he addresses homosexuality that was an issue in 1st century Rome and was an issue for Paul. In the Rome of Paul's day, homosexuality was often an expression of authority that men exercised over slave boys. Even before Christianity became a major force in Roman culture, physicians cautioned men about homosexuality for reasons of physical and mental health.

From his Jewish heritage, Paul had a negative view of homosexuality. His understanding of love reflected in the teachings and relationships of Jesus also shaped his perspective. He viewed the prevailing practices of ancient Rome as unacceptable for Christians.

[Romans 1:24-32]

- According to Paul, how does God view homosexuality?
- How should Christians today respond to Paul's views expressed in this passage?
- What is your view of a "Christian marriage"?

FOR FURTHER DISCUSSION OR PERSONAL REFLECTION:

[ROMANS 1]

What do you think it must have been like to belong to the early Christian church?

Would you sign up for membership in a church like that?

[ROMANS 1:16]

Have you ever been ashamed of the Gospel? Clarify.

How is the Gospel of Jesus "Good News" for all who believe it?

SESSION 2

WHAT IS GOD'S RIGHTEOUS JUDGEMENT?
Romans 2:1-3:20

After painting a dark picture of the condition of men and women who turn their backs on God, Paul warns against judging others because those who pass judgment do the same things as those they are judging and thus condemn themselves. Don't think, Paul adds, that God's judgment will be escaped!

"Do you show contempt for the riches of [God's] kindness, tolerance and patience, not realizing that God's kindness leads you towards repentance? Because of your stubbornness and your unrepentant heart, you are storing up wrath against yourself for the day of God's wrath, when his righteous judgment will be revealed."

[Romans 2:4,5]

- What does "repentance" mean?
- Have you experienced God's kindness leading you to repentance? If so, how?

Paul uses the term "righteousness" to identify a right relationship with God and an ethical (or right) way of living. The righteousness God imparted through the death and resurrection of Jesus, acquits people of that for which they are guilty. They are no longer condemned.

Paul will come back to this theme throughout his letter. He will also explain that for any of us to benefit from this acquittal, we must acknowledge our sin—everything we have done in violation of God's law—and accept God's grace. He will further explain that we will want to show our gratitude for the gift of righteousness by loving our fellow humans irrespective of their race, religion, gender or station in life.

In Paul's day the Jewish law included the Ten Commandments and many additional requirements. When the early church's mission was extended to non-Jews, someone had to clarify their relationship to the laws of Judaism (the religion of the Jews). Paul did that. He made these points.

One: Those who merely hear the Law are not righteous in God's sight. Those who obey the Law will be declared righteous. When Gentiles (non-Jews), who do not have the Law, do what is required by the Law, they show that the requirements of the Law are written on their hearts.

Two: Being Jewish is nothing to brag about if you don't walk the talk of the Jewish faith. "A man is not a Jew if he is only one outwardly . . ." (Romans 2:28) Paul lectured Jewish members of the Christian church in Rome that if they made a big deal about their relationship to God based on their Law and felt qualified to be guides to the blind, they may well trip over their own self-righteousness.

> - **What is the basis of a righteous relationship with God?**
> - **Do you enjoy that relationship now? If so, how?**

According to Jewish Law in Paul's time, all Jewish males were required to be circumcised. This rite was a ticket into the official ranks of Judaism and was deemed an important act of obedience to the Law. Paul reminded Jewish Christians that this was important only if it reflected the internal commitment of men so marked. It was about the heart not the body.

A man was a Jew, Paul said, if he was one inwardly, and circumcision was circumcision of the heart, by the Spirit, not by the written code. Paul added these thoughts about being a Jewish Christian: There is an advantage for Jews who become Christians. They had been entrusted with the very words of God (the Hebrew Bible – what Christians call the Old Testament). Those words were planted in their culture. But Paul was clear that both Jews with their special heritage and Gentiles without that special heritage alike fall short of God's calling. Thus no one would be declared righteous in God's sight by observing the Law; rather, through the Law we become aware of sin, because you can only know that you fall short if there is a standard.

[Romans 2:6-29]

- If you were a Gentile Christian in the early Christian church, how would you feel about living by the legal code of Judaism (that, besides the Ten Commandments, included scores of regulations on the types of foods that could be eaten, clothes that could be worn, etc.)?

- What does it mean for the Law to be written on the heart?

- What outward forms of religion today compare with circumcision?

- If God's Truth has been planted in our culture, what responsibilities do we have for that?

Paul draws on his knowledge of the Jewish writing to show what he is saying is not a new idea, but a recurring theme from ancient writers. "There is no one righteous, not even one; there is no one who understands, no one who seeks God." (Romans 3:10) He summarizes his quoting from Psalms and Ecclesiastes by explaining that no one can live up to the letter of the Law, but the law is useful because it makes us become conscious of our sin.

[Romans 3:1-20]

FOR FURTHER DISCUSSION OR PERSONAL REFLECTION:

[ROMANS 2:1-3:20]

Why does focusing on outward forms of religious practice have such a strong attraction?

What marks in your own life reflect your internal commitment to God?

How would you assess the balance between outward forms of religious practice and internal commitment in your own life?

What evidence is there that God's Truth has been planted in our culture?

If God's Truth has been planted in our culture, what responsibilities do we have for that?

SESSION 3

WHAT IS THE WAY TO BE RIGHT WITH GOD?

Romans 3:21-4:25

For Jews, righteousness with God came from strict observance of the Law. This was not very good news because perfect observance of the Law was not only onerous but impossible! Paul found in Jesus the Good News about a righteousness from God.

> "But now a righteousness from God, separate from the law, has been made known, to which the Law and the Prophets testify. This righteousness from God comes through faith in Jesus Christ to all who believe."
>
> [Romans 3:21,22]

As Paul explains this righteousness, he incorporates four terms that once understood help illuminate his writing. These definitions are adapted from Alan Richardson's *Theological Word Book of the Bible*:

Justify/Justification — Justification is the first step in the process of salvation, that first reconciliation to God which is the beginning of a steady growth in grace and in the knowledge of God. It is that immediate *setting right with God* that is accomplished by God's grace when a person has faith.

Grace — God's redemptive love that is always active to save sinners and maintain their relationship with God. Grace is God's covenant-love, which has broken down all barriers. Grace is a free gift of God.

Redeem/Redemption — This term comes from the practice of buying back something that formerly belonged to the purchaser but for some reason passed out of his possession. It also conveys the idea of paying the price required to secure a benefit and comes from the same root as the word ransom. In the New Testament, redemption results in cleansing from guilt and releasing from the power of sin. It brings the knowledge of forgiveness and delivers one from alienation to God.

Atonement — A covering of sins whereby they are treated as nonexistent and the sinner as if he had not committed them. Faith in God through Jesus Christ extracts the root of sin and frees up the process of healing.

"All have sinned and fall short of the glory of God, and are justified freely by his grace through the redemption that came by Christ Jesus." Paul added: "God presented Jesus as a sacrifice for the atonement of sin to those who have faith in his blood. He did this to demonstrate his justice… [that] justifies those who have faith in Jesus."

"We maintain that [one] is justified by faith apart from observing the Law." By "Law" Paul meant both the standards for behavior that God gave through Moses and also the distortion of that Law when it was used as a basis for self-righteousness. "God justifies Jews and Gentiles through faith in Jesus. Do we, then, nullify the Law by this faith? Not at all! Rather, we uphold the Law."

Paul wrote this against the backdrop of serious conflict in many of the early Christian congregations over whether Christians were required to keep the Law. He suffered considerable abuse from Jewish Christians who believed that God demanded that Christians observe the traditions of Judaism (the Law).

[Romans 3:21-31]

- What did Paul mean when he said that God's justice justifies those who have faith in Jesus?
- What did being a Christian mean to Paul?
- To what extent do you believe Christianity is based on faith in Christ, and to what extent is it based on behavior (i.e., obedience to God's laws)?
- How does your belief influence your day-to-day life?

Abraham was the forefather of the Jews, a man called a "friend of God." Was Abraham justified (set right with God) by works—by his good deeds? Paul said, "No." Rather: "Abraham believed God, and it was credited to him as righteousness."

Paul quoted a psalm of David. "Blessed are they whose transgressions are forgiven, whose sins are covered. Blessed is the man whose sin the Lord will never count against him." (Psalm 32:1,2) Paul cited King David as one who found the basis for salvation in God's grace rather than in works based on obedience to the Law. Paul told the Christians in Rome that Abraham was the father not only of the Jews. Abraham is the father of all who believe.

[Romans 4:1-12]

Then Paul made a claim that must have shocked Jewish Christians. It was not through the Law that Abraham and his offspring received the promise that he would be heir of the world but through the righteousness that comes by faith.

Paul reminded his readers that Abraham was called to be the father of many nations when he was very old (99) and his wife Sarah was well beyond the normal childbearing age (89). It took quite a leap of faith for Abraham to believe that God could deliver on the promise to extend his family at that stage of his life.

"Against all hope, Abraham in hope believed and so became the father of many nations." Paul added that Abraham was fully persuaded that God had power to do what he had promised. His faith was credited to him as righteousness.

Paul then affirmed that the same relationship with God is available to each of us. "God will credit righteousness for all of us who believe in him who raised Jesus our Lord from the dead—who was raised to life for our justification."

[Romans 4:13-25]

Paul concluded that the promise God made to Abraham came by faith so that it would be by grace (a free gift apart from obedience to the Law). Abraham is the father of us all—those who are of the Law and those who are of the faith.

- If Abraham and David were justified by faith and not by works, why did Jesus need to appear and atone for our sin?
- What does it mean to have a trusting faith in God?
- What do you consider as the basis of your right relationship with God?

FOR FURTHER DISCUSSION OR PERSONAL REFLECTION:

[ROMANS: 3-23]
If there is only one God, do all religions lead to God? Why or why not?

To what extent do you believe Christianity is based on faith in Christ, and to what extent is it based on behavior (i.e., obedience to God's laws)?

[ROMANS 4]
Jews, Muslims, and Christians are descendants of Abraham. How do you account for the apparent lack of unity among these descendants today?

What seems to be the major differences in the "faith" expressed by these three religious groups?

What *should* be the relationship today among Abraham's descendants?

Paul wrote that faith is *credited* as righteousness. What does this mean?

Where does hope fit in with your faith in God?

SESSION 4

WHAT COMES WITH PEACE WITH GOD?
Romans 5:1-21

Having shown that man is justified, (brought into right-standing with God) through faith in chapters 1-4, Paul declares: "we have peace with God through our Lord Jesus Christ, through whom we have gained access by faith into this grace in which we now stand." This peace, or reconciliation with God, came at a great price.

"You see, at just the right time, when we were still powerless, Christ died for the ungodly. Very rarely will anyone die for a righteous person, though for a good person someone might possibly dare to die. But God demonstrates his own love for us in this: While we were still sinners, Christ died for us."

[Romans 5:1-8]

- What does it mean to have "peace with God"?

"For if, when we were God's enemies, we were reconciled to him through the death of his Son, how much more, having been reconciled, shall we be saved through his life!"

- How were we enemies of God?
- What does it mean to be reconciled to God?
- What does it mean to share God's life?

Paul shows how death entered the world through the sin of the first man, Adam, and how that death affects everyone born since that time. He contrasts that death with the life brought through the death of Jesus. "For just as through the disobedience of the one man the many were made sinners, so also through the obedience of the one man (Jesus) the many will be made righteous."

[Romans 5:9-19]

- What relationship do you feel between the death of Christ and your experience of God's love?

We can rejoice in God through our Lord Jesus Christ through whom we now have been reconciled. Sin reigned in death. Grace reigns through righteousness. This brings eternal life through Jesus Christ our Lord.

[Romans 5:20, 21]

FOR FURTHER DISCUSSION OR PERSONAL REFLECTION:

[ROMANS 5:1-5]

For whom would you be willing to die? Why?

Do you have peace with God? If so, describe what it means in your life.

Have there been times when your suffering produced perseverance? What did that feel like?

SESSION 5

WHAT DRIVES SPIRITUAL TRANSFORMATION?

Romans 6:1-23

"What shall we say, then? Shall we go on sinning so that grace may increase? By no means! We are those who have died to sin; how can we live in it any longer?" Paul begins chapter 6 with a series of questions that demand answers from every believer. ". . . don't you know that all of us who were baptized into Christ Jesus were baptized into his death? We were therefore buried with him through baptism into death in order that, just as Christ was raised from the dead through the glory of the Father, we too may live a new life."

[Romans 6:1-4]

- What is the grace that Paul writes about?
- How would more sinning increase this grace?
- Why does Paul condemn this idea?

Paul implores the Romans to understand that they are united with Christ in death and therefore should no longer be slaves to sin—"because anyone who has died has been set free from sin." Explaining that Christ has already died for our sins, Paul writes, "do not let sin reign in your mortal body so that you obey its evil desires. Do not offer any part of yourself to sin as an instrument of wickedness, but rather offer yourselves to God as those who have been brought from death to life...For sin shall no longer be your master, because you are not under the law, but under grace."

[Romans 6:5-14]

- Is it a choice to allow sin to be your master?
- How does giving our lives to Christ affect that choice?

Paul again asks the question that he asked at the beginning of the chapter contrasting life under the law to life under grace. He answers it by evoking the image of slavery, or what we might think of as voluntary indentured servitude. "When you offer yourselves to someone as obedient slaves, you are slaves of the one you obey—whether you are slaves to sin, which leads to death, or to obedience, which leads to righteousness." Paul wants Roman Christians as well as all Christ followers to understand that they have been set free from sin and instead have chosen to become people who live in right standing before God.

[Romans 6:15-18]

- How does obeying the law make one a slave to the law?

"I am using an example from everyday life because of your human limitations. Just as you used to offer yourselves as slaves to impurity and to ever-increasing wickedness, so now offer yourselves as slaves to righteousness leading to holiness. When you were slaves to sin, you were free from the control of righteousness. What benefit did you reap at that time from the things you are now ashamed of? Those things result in death! But now that you have been set free from sin and have become slaves of God, the benefit you reap leads to holiness, and the result is eternal life.

- What in your life has caused you shame?
- How have you been set free from that shame?

Paul closes this chapter with one of the most challenging and at the same time, most hopeful verses in the Bible. "For the wages of sin is death, but the gift of God is eternal life in Christ Jesus our Lord."

[Romans 6:19-23]

- Why does Paul compare wages with a gift?

FOR FURTHER DISCUSSION OR PERSONAL REFLECTION:

[ROMANS 6:1-25]

What does it mean to be united with Christ in his resurrection?

What does it mean to be alive to God in Christ Jesus?

[ROMANS 6:3]

Why is baptism like dying with Christ?

Is baptism a requirement for being a Christian? Why or why not?

[ROMANS 6:22, 23]

How do you see yourself moving from "slavery to sin" to a voluntary indentured servant to righteousness? What does that look like?

SESSION 6

WHAT IS THE RELATIONSHIP BETWEEN THE LAW AND SIN?

Romans 7:1-8:16

Those who are in bondage to sin, often tell Christians that it is the believers who are in bondage. They seem to think that a set of rules and regulations restrict the freedom of Christians. Such is the blinding effect of sin. Those who engage in a life of sin are slaves to the things that they think they enjoy. From their perspective, they misunderstand the true freedom that comes about by placing faith in Christ as savior and lord. This subtle lie of Satan will cause many to reject Christ, the only source of true freedom.

In Paul's culture, a married woman was bound to her husband as long as he was alive, but if her husband died, she was released from the law of marriage. Paul conveyed through this analogy that we were once married to sin, but when the power of sin died we were freed to marry another and, in this case, a better spouse, Jesus, the Christ. "When we die to the law, we belong to him who was raised from the dead in order that we might bear fruit to God."

For Paul, it was important that the old life burdened with sin and bridled by the constraints of legalism be put to rest. Then the renewing powers of grace and the freedom of redeeming love that emerge from bonding with Christ could forge believers into new creations to become what God created them to be.

[Romans 7:1-13]

- What does it mean to "belong" to Jesus?
- If you have bonded with Jesus, from what have you been released?
- What is meant by the freedom of redeeming love?

John Knox in *The Interpreters' Bible* wrote: "Much of Romans is concerned with setting forth the nature of the new life. The key term is 'Spirit.' The new life is spiritual life— God's own life imparted to us, and therefore our own true life, since in the beginning he made us by breathing his Spirit upon us. This Spirit, who is love, brings reconciliation within and without, or what Paul calls 'peace.' The Spirit also brings powerful reinforcement to our own 'spirit' so that we are able to triumph over the sinful desires of the flesh and to know something of the original order and peace of God's creation.

- If you wished to convey to another person the deeper meaning of Paul's marriage analogy, how would you describe the benefits of this bonding to Jesus?
- What "fruit to God" might we bear as a result of bonding with Jesus?

'Paul was a student of the rabbis of Orthodox Judaism. His view of sin reflected their teachings. They taught that we are subject to a God-given inclination that can lead either to good or to evil. If not directed by a will informed by God's law, this inclination was directed by the will that leads to sin. This inclination is a basic energy or desire present in everyone. In the next segment, Paul described the conflict we experience when this inclination is not aligned with God's will.

"What I want to do I do not do, but what I hate I do." God's Law provides a standard by which this inclination can be checked and directed. When we are one with the Christ by faith, we are aligned with God's will and directed away from our inclination to sin. This transformation occurs not as a rational act of the will but as a gift of God's grace through Jesus, God's Anointed One. Through him this powerful inclination is brought into harmony and wholeness. Paul summarizes this harmonization of the ongoing dilemma: "Thanks be to God, who delivers me through Jesus Christ our Lord! So then, I myself in my mind am a slave to God's law, but in my sinful nature a slave to the law of sin."

[Romans 7:14-25]

> **How does one reconcile being a slave to two masters: God's law and the law of sin?**

Those who live according to their sinful nature have their minds set on what that nature desires; but those who live in accordance with the Spirit have their minds set on what the Spirit desires. "The Spirit himself testifies with our spirit that we are God's children." Paul proclaimed that not only are we rescued from sin and death and have the Spirit of God within us, we are God's children—heirs of God and co-heirs with Christ. If we share in Christ's sufferings, we share also in his glory.

[Romans 8:1-16]

- How do you know if and when the Spirit of God lives in you?
- What does it mean to share in the glory of God?

FOR FURTHER DISCUSSION OR PERSONAL REFLECTION:

[ROMANS 8:5-8]

How would you describe the "mindset" that guides your life?

How is harmony achieved in a group of people with different mindsets?

What that you have heard from Paul so far that might upset the harmony in the congregation in Rome?

[ROMANS 7:1 – 8:16]

Do you have any new understandings of what Paul meant by being a Christian? If so, what are they?

[ROMANS 8:14]

What does it mean to be God's children?

Do you feel like a child of God? If so, what does that mean to you?

How should this image of God's family influence Christians?

SESSION 7

HOW DO WE SHARE IN CHRIST'S GLORY?
Romans 8:17-39

Looking back on Romans 7 we see that the Law and its synonyms are mentioned more than 30 times, and the Holy Spirit just once (in verse 6). By contrast, in Romans 8 Paul places most of his emphasis on the work of the Spirit. He shows how the law is weak when compared to the power of the Spirit. Now Paul turns his attention from the work of the Holy Spirit in the present to the glory of God's children in the future.

Paul declared that our present sufferings are nothing compared with the glory that will be revealed in us. The creation will be liberated from its bondage to decay and brought into the glorious freedom of the children of God.

New Testament scholar J.B. Phillips captured Paul's spirit in his translation. "The whole creation is on tiptoe to see the wonderful sight of the [children] of God coming into their own."

- We have every reason to be hopeful.
- The Spirit will help us in our weakness.
- The Spirit will help us to pray for what we ought to pray for.
- God works for the good of those who love him, who are called according to his purpose.

[Romans 8:18, 28]

> - **Paul said God works for the good of those who love him and who are called according to his purpose. Do you feel called according to God's purpose? If so, describe the feeling.**
>
> - **Have you discovered the purpose for which you were created? If so, what is it and how did you discover it?**

We must now deal with a tough section from Paul's letter that has caused considerable discussion and debate. Sincere people take different sides of what these words mean. Keep the whole picture that Paul paints in mind. "For those God foreknew he also predestined to be conformed to the likeness of his Son, that he might be the firstborn among many brothers. And those he predestined, he also called; those he called, he also justified; those he justified, he also glorified."

Several of the terms Paul used in this passage have been interpreted in different ways making clarity on the issue a real challenge. Among these are predestination, election, and foreordination. When God speaks through the scriptures, God's self and God's Truth are revealed through multiple channels to make clear that which is to be conveyed. To understand what God meant we must look at these words of Paul in the context of other words he wrote. To gain perspective on what Paul wished to convey keep in mind what he disclosed in previous segments of his letter and what you will discover in the segments to follow.

> **What questions would you like to ask Paul about the passage above?**

Some thoughtful students of the Bible take the position that God chooses some to share the inheritance in Christ whereas others are not on that invitation list. Others take the position that God wants all of us to experience the acceptance (by grace through faith) made clear in the life, sacrificial and atoning death, and triumphant resurrection of Jesus, God's Son and Anointed One. The coming of Jesus was to make explicit the depth and inclusiveness of God's love. Jews and Gentiles alike are included. Those who respond will be transformed to the likeness of Christ. God also endowed us with the freedom to say "No thanks!" and to carve out our own approach to a life that ignores God's Lordship.

> **Do you feel you are on God's invitation list? Based on what?**
>
> **What role does freedom to accept or not to accept God's acceptance of us have in God's plan of salvation?**

What Paul wrote next helps us gain a perspective. "Who shall separate us from the love of Christ? Shall trouble or hardship or persecution or famine or nakedness or danger or sword? No, in all these things we are more than conquerors through him who loved us."

- What is it that we who are "more than conquerors" are to conquer?

- When have you felt that you were "more than a conqueror" through Jesus Christ?

Paul, in one of the most powerful affirmations in his letters, declares that nothing is able to separate us from the love of God.

"For I am convinced that neither death nor life, neither angels nor demons, neither the present nor the future, nor any powers, neither height nor depth, nor anything else in all creation, will be able to separate us from the love of God that is in Christ Jesus our Lord."

[Romans 8:38,39]

FOR FURTHER DISCUSSION OR PERSONAL REFLECTION:

[PAUL 8:18-21]
What does "the glorious freedom of the children of God" mean?

What does the liberation of the creation from the bondage of decay mean?

[ROMANS 8:26]
Paul said that the Spirit will help us in our weakness. Has the Spirit helped you in your weakness? If so, how?

[ROMANS 8:38,39]
What is needed for you to feel that nothing can ever separate you from the love of God?

[ROMANS 8]
What would be the impact on the society in which you live if Christian congregations reflected the triumphant life Paul described?

SESSION 8

IS THERE HOPE FOR THE JEWS?
Romans 9:1-10:4

Paul's concern for the role of the Jews in God's plan was personal. Not only was he, like most of the early believers, a Jew by birth and upbringing, he was a Jewish scholar and zealot for Judaism. By the middle of the 1st century many Christians were scattered around the world. Many Jewish leaders, including Paul, saw in the early believers a threat to their historic, law-based religion. Paul witnessed with approval the execution by stoning of Stephen, a passionate preacher of the Gospel of Jesus. The religious leaders commissioned Paul to stamp out this Christian heresy, but Paul became a follower of Christ. Now he looks with pain and great concern for his Jewish brethren who have not decided to follow Jesus.

> "I could wish that I myself were cursed and cut off from Christ for the sake of my brothers, those of my own race, the people of Israel. Theirs is the adoption as sons, theirs the divine glory, the covenants, the receiving of the Law, the temple worship and the promises. Theirs are the patriarchs, and from them is traced the human ancestry of Christ, who is God over all, forever praised!"
>
> [Romans 9:1-5]

> **Jews and Christians worship God in different ways. How do you think God prefers to be worshipped?**

Paul affirmed that things happened in the history of the Jews so that God's purpose in election might stand. He reminded them that God's promise to Abraham was carried down through his son, Isaac. When Isaac's wife delivered twins, it was the second to be born that God chose to carry on the promise, changing that son's name from Jacob to Israel. Paul writes of Jacob's mother, "Rebekah's children were conceived at the same time by our father Isaac. Yet, before the twins were born or had done anything good or bad—in order that God's purpose in election might stand: not by works but by him who calls—she was told, *'The older will serve the younger.'* Just as it is written: *'Jacob I loved, but Esau I hated.'"*

[Romans 9:6-13]

> **How do we reconcile the idea that humans have free will but God makes choices on our behalf?**

Paul also reminded the Romans that God told Moses: "I will have mercy on whom I have mercy and I will have compassion on whom I have compassion." (Exodus 33:19) He explained that "It does not depend on man's desire or effort, but on God's mercy." He then cited Exodus again to show's God sovereignty when the Pharaoh, the King of Egypt, received God's Word: "I raised you up for this purpose, that I might display my power in you and that my name might be proclaimed in all the earth."(Exodus 9:16)

> Did God promote evil actions against Egypt? Would that run contrary to God's nature?

Paul concluded that just as the potter has the right to fashion pottery for noble and for common uses, so God had the right to grant Gentiles a righteousness based on their faith and to allow Israel (the Jews) to pursue a course based on works – even though that course of action proved to be a stumbling block.

[Romans 9:14-33]

> What can Christians learn from the history of the Jews?
>
> Is God's plan of salvation different for Jews than for Gentiles? How would Paul answer that question?

FOR FURTHER DISCUSSION OR PERSONAL REFLECTION:

[ROMANS 9]

If a Jew sought to win you to Judaism, how would you respond?

Does God see either Jews or Christians as a "chosen people"? Why or why not?

Do Christians have any responsibility for protecting the Jewish state of Israel? Why?

SESSION 9

WHAT IS THE MESSAGE OF SALVATION TO ALL?

Romans 10:1 – 11:36

"Brothers and sisters, my heart's desire and prayer to God for the Israelites is that they may be saved," writes Paul passionately. "For I can testify about them that they are zealous for God, but their zeal is not based on knowledge. Since they did not know the righteousness of God and sought to establish their own, they did not submit to God's righteousness. Christ is the culmination of the law so that there may be righteousness for everyone who believes."

[Romans 10:1-4]

Paul lays out his thesis and then defends it in chapters 10 and 11. The word of faith proclaimed by Paul is this: If you confess with your mouth, "Jesus is Lord," and believe in your heart that God raised him from the dead you will be saved. Lest there be any doubt, Paul reiterates in verse 13, "Everyone who calls on the name of the Lord will be saved."

- What does it mean to be saved?

Paul then asked, "How can they believe in the one of whom they have not heard? And how can they hear without someone preaching to them?" Paul quoted from the prophet Isaiah, "How beautiful are the feet of those who bring good news!" He wanted to remind the Roman Christians that the Jewish people had been given many opportunities to hear and respond to the call of God, but failed to do so. Paul quoted a lament from the writings of Isaiah: "All day long I have held out my hands to a disobedient and obstinate people." (Isaiah 65:2)

[Romans 10:5-21]

> Are you able to say, "Jesus is Lord?" Clarify what this means to you.

Did God reject his people? By no means! Even though they resisted the guidance of prophets such as Isaiah, God chose a remnant – a portion of the people who remained faithful. Throughout history, God found those who understood divine Truth. God used even the resistance of the Jews to expand the reach of the Gospel to Gentiles. Paul wrote the Jews' loss meant riches for the Gentiles, and he added: "how much greater riches will their fullness bring!"

[Romans 11:1-12]

> What did Paul mean by "how much greater riches will their fullness bring"?

By opening the path of righteousness to Gentiles, God could arouse his own people (the Jews) to follow that path. If the Jews' rejection of The Way led to the reconciliation of the world, what might their acceptance lead to? Israel experienced a hardening until Gentiles were empowered by the Gospel to become a part of God's chosen people. But now: "All Israel will be saved." God's gifts and God's call are irrevocable.

[Romans 11:13-26]

> ■ What is Paul's understanding of God's strategy to save the world?

Paul concludes this section of his letter with a doxology or short hymn of praise to God. He borrows phrases from Old Testament writers to encourage the church in Rome.

Oh, the depth of the riches of the wisdom and knowledge of God!
    How unsearchable his judgments,
    and his paths beyond tracing out!
"Who has known the mind of the Lord?
    Or who has been his counselor?"
"Who has ever given to God,
    that God should repay them?"
For from him and through him and for him are all things.
    To him be the glory forever! Amen.

[Romans 11:33-36]

> ■ What thoughts and feelings come to mind as you read this 2000-year old doxology?

FOR FURTHER DISCUSSION OR PERSONAL REFLECTION:

[ROMANS 10:12,13]
How might members of the Roman church respond to Paul's contention: that "there is no difference between Jew and Gentile—the same Lord is Lord of all and richly blesses all who call on him, for (as the Jewish prophet Joel has written), 'Everyone who calls on the name of the Lord will be saved.'"

[ROMANS 10]
What would a church that effectively demonstrated God's good news look like?

Would you want to be a member of such a church? Why or why not?

What forces restrain churches from effectively demonstrating God's good news?

[ROMANS 11:1-5]
What "remnants" (before and after Christ) kept the faith?

[ROMANS 11:25-36]
When was Paul expecting that "all Israel will be saved"?

Would you be comfortable discussing these views of Paul with your Jewish friends? Why or why not?

SESSION 10

WHAT DOES SERIOUS LOVE CALL FOR?

Romans 12:1-13:14

Paul called the Romans, and by extension all Christ followers, to respond to God's gracious act of love. "Offer your bodies as a living sacrifice, holy and pleasing to God—this is your true and proper worship," Paul wrote. Then he explained living sacrifice. "Do not conform to the pattern of this world, but be transformed by the renewing of your mind. Then you will be able to test and approve what God's will is—his good, pleasing and perfect will."

[Romans 12:1,2]

- What do you think Paul meant when he said "be transformed by the renewing of your mind"?
- Do you feel transformed by the renewal of your mind? If so, what led you to that transformation?
- What happens if we allow the world to conform us to its pattern?

Paul followed his call for a living sacrifice by laying out a code of behavior that is in harmony with the teachings of Jesus. He also quotes passages from the Old Testament to drive home his points.

- Don't think of yourself more highly than you ought.
- Think of yourself with sober judgment, in accordance with the measure of faith God gave you.
- Just as our physical bodies have many members with different functions, so in Christ all believers are one body and each member belongs to all the others.
- There are many gifts among us, such as: prophesy, service, teaching, encouraging, contributing to the needs of others, leadership, and showing mercy. Each of us is called to make the most of the unique gifts God has given us.
- Love with sincerity.
- Hate what is evil.
- Cling to what is good.
- Be devoted to one another in love.
- Honor one another above yourselves.
- Don't lack in zeal but keep your spiritual fervor in the service of the Lord.
- Be joyful in hope, patient in affliction, and faithful in prayer.
- Share with God's people who are in need.
- Practice hospitality.
- Bless rather than curse those who persecute you.
- Rejoice with those who rejoice.
- Mourn with those who mourn.
- Live in harmony with one another.

- Do not be proud, but be willing to associate with people of low position.
- Do not be conceited.
- Don't repay evil with evil.
- Do what is right in the eyes of all.
- As far as it depends on you, live at peace with everyone.
- Do not take revenge — leave that to God. (Deuteronomy 32:35)
- Show compassion to your enemies. (Proverbs 25:21,22)
- Don't be overcome by evil — overcome evil with good.

[Romans 12:3-21]

- Paul said that in Christ we are one body and each member belongs to all the others. What does this mean for you in your relationships?
- What gifts has God given you? How are you using these gifts?

Paul said everyone must submit to the governing authorities because God established them. "Those who rebel against authority rebel against what God instituted. Rulers hold no terror for those who do right, but for those who do wrong. This is why you pay taxes, for the authorities are God's servants, who give their full time to governing."

[Romans 13:1-6]

> - What authorities do you believe are God's servants?
> - What is the role of individual Christians, congregations, and/or other religious organizations to influence governing authorities?

"Let no debt remain outstanding, except the continuing debt to love one another, for he who loves his fellowman has fulfilled the Law. The commandments, 'Do not commit adultery,' 'Do not murder,' 'Do not steal,' 'Do not covet,' and whatever other commandment there may be, are summed up in this one rule: 'Love your neighbor as yourself.' Love does no harm to its neighbor. Therefore love is the fulfillment of the Law."

[Romans 13:8-10]

Note: In *The Four Loves*, British author and theologian C.S. Lewis distinguished between Need-love and Gift-love. Gift-love longs to serve and is willing to suffer for another. It is Need-love that draws us to God and that draws the infant to its mother. Need-love can draw us to sources of compassion and renewal. Need-love tends to last only as long as the need exists. On the other hand, Gift-love tends to endure. Lewis viewed God as the ultimate expression of love. God-Love is the ultimate Gift-love. In this love, wrote Lewis, "there is no hunger that needs to be filled; only plenteousness that desires to give." Gift-love simply desires what is best for the beloved. This love enables us to love what is not naturally lovable. It even enables us to have a Gift-love for ourselves.

> **Does Paul's summary of the commandments make it easier or more difficult for you to obey the will of God? Explain.**

Paul concludes chapter 13 by reminding the Romans to recognize that there is no time like the present to live into the life that God wants for us, putting aside "the deeds of darkness" and putting on "the armor of light." After describing deeds of darkness, he calls on the Christians to "clothe yourselves with the Lord Jesus Christ, and do not think about how to gratify the desires of the flesh."

[Romans 13:11-14]

FOR FURTHER DISCUSSION OR PERSONAL REFLECTION:

[ROMANS 12:9]
What are ways you can overcome evil with good?

[ROMANS 12:3-21]
What barriers prevent you from practicing your faith fully?

[ROMANS 12:16]
In what areas of your life do you find it most difficult to live in harmony with others?

[ROMANS 13:1-7]
When might it be right to rebel against a governing authority?

What forms of rebellion is it right to exercise against a governing authority?

How do you express your Christian citizenship?

[ROMANS 13:9]
What is the difference between loving yourself and being arrogant or "self-centered"?

What barriers do you face in loving your neighbor as yourself?

What are the benefits of loving your neighbor as yourself?

What could you do, beginning now, to love your neighbors more?

SESSION 11

HOW DO WE LIVE THE EXAMPLE OF CHRIST?
Romans 14:23

"Accept the one whose faith is weak, without quarreling over disputable matters. One man's faith allows him to eat everything, but another man, whose faith is weak, eats only vegetables." In Paul's day a controversy arose over eating certain foods. Jewish Christians refrained from eating foods prohibited by Old Testament laws and foods that had been offered to Roman gods and idols. Most Gentile Christians saw no harm in this. Paul said if we distress one another with certain "controversial" behaviors we are not acting in love.

[Romans 14:1-18]

- What are some differences among Christians today that lead to intolerance among fellow Christians?
- Why are we judgmental toward those who hold views different from ours?

"Let us therefore make every effort to do what leads to peace and to mutual edification. Do not destroy the work of God for the sake of food. All food is clean, but it is wrong for a person to eat anything that causes someone else to stumble. It is better not to eat meat or drink wine or to do anything else that will cause your brother or sister to fall."

Though the focus here is food sacrificed to idols, Paul urged believers not to exercise their right to do something controversial if, by doing so, they destroy the work of God. We may compare these issues with today's differences in attitudes about social drinking, modes of dress, Sabbath observance, and the use of profanity among church goers. It was better, Paul argued, not to engage in controversial practices that offended or caused fellow Christians to fall. But Paul reminded them: "The Kingdom of God is not a matter of eating and drinking, but of righteousness, peace and joy in the Holy Spirit."

[Romans 14:19-23]

- How inclusive and "tolerant" should we be in our religious communities?
- What principles must be honored and practiced in congregations to prevent rituals from being divisive?

Paul calls on strong believers to do something that seems contrary to human nature, "bear with the failings of the weak and not to please ourselves. Each of us should please our neighbors for their good, to build them up." He then reminds the Roman church that Christ did not do what pleased himself but took on our insults . . . our sins. By these actions, Jesus brought about the hope that was central to the message of the Old Testament.

This reminder flows into an encouraging benediction: "May the God who gives endurance and encouragement give you the same attitude of mind toward each other that Christ Jesus had, so that with one mind and one voice you may glorify the God and Father of our Lord Jesus Christ."

[Romans 15:1-6]

- How should Christians accept and care for the weak in faith?
- How will living out this challenge bring about a single mindedness that glorifies God?

Paul's benediction continues as he issues another plea for acceptance of one another "just as Christ accepted you." He then quotes Old Testament scripture to affirm the Gentiles' place in God's kingdom, and offers this blessing: "May the God of hope fill you with all joy and peace as you trust in him, so that you may overflow with hope by the power of the Holy Spirit."

[Romans 15:7-13]

FOR FURTHER DISCUSSION OR PERSONAL REFLECTION:

[ROMANS 14:13]

How should Christians accept and care for the weak in faith?

What can you do to enable people to be strong in their faith?

[ROMANS 14:13-21]

Paul defined what it meant to be a member of a Christian community. Would you sign up for membership in a congregation such as he describes? Why or why not?

[ROMANS 15:7]

What does being accepted by Christ mean to you?

How do the believers with whom you associate demonstrate Christ-like acceptance of others?

[ROMANS 15:13]

Is your church filled with joy and peace? Is it overflowing with hope?

What can you do to encourage your church family?

SESSION 12

HOW DO YOU CLOSE A LETTER LIKE PAUL'S TO THE ROMANS?

Romans 15:14-16:27

After so many instructions and admonitions, we might be surprised to read what Paul wrote in the closing section of his letter. "I myself am convinced, my brothers, that you yourselves are full of goodness, complete in knowledge and competent to instruct one another."

He offered this credential for his mission: "I glory in Christ Jesus in my service to God. I will not venture to speak of anything except what Christ has accomplished through me in leading the Gentiles to obey God by what I have said and done — by the power of signs and miracles, through the power of the Spirit." And, Paul apologized for having been hindered from visiting the Christians in Rome. He had been busy in his efforts to reach those in places where Christ was not known. "It has always been my ambition to preach the gospel where Christ was not known, so that I would not be building on someone else's foundation."

[Romans 15:14-20]

> - If the Christians in Rome were full of goodness, complete in knowledge, and competent to instruct one another, what else would they need to be a strong congregation?
> - Paul felt that Jesus was not properly represented in many early church congregations. In what ways do you think Jesus is not properly represented in current church congregations?

Paul was something of a diplomat or politician. He used various tactics to secure the support he needed. He alienated some of the early church leaders in Jerusalem with his approach to his mission. As he traveled to reach Gentiles, Paul gathered funds to assist the poor among the Christians in Jerusalem. Paul believed that since Gentiles shared in the Jews' spiritual blessings, they needed to share their own material blessings with their Jewish Christian brothers and sisters. Paul added: "So after I have completed this task and have made sure that they have received this fruit, I will go to Spain and visit you on the way."

[Romans 15:21-29]

> - The Jewish Christians in Jerusalem caused Paul considerable grief. Here he refers to them as "the saints in Jerusalem." (The word "saint" suggests holiness from God.) How do you account for Paul's caring intercession on the part of those who were highly critical of him?

Paul urged the Roman Christians to join him in his "struggle" to spread the Gospel of Christ against opposition from unbelievers. "I urge you, brothers, by our Lord Jesus Christ and by the love of the Spirit, to join me in my struggle by praying to God for me. Pray that I may be rescued from the unbelievers in Judea and that my service in Jerusalem may be acceptable to the saints there, so that by God's will I may come to you with joy and together with you be refreshed. The God of peace be with you all."

[Romans 15:30-33]

- In his internal and external struggle, Paul invoked the God of peace to be with the Roman Christians. What did he mean by the God of "peace"?

- In his spiritual transformation Paul found new life. How would you describe that new life?

Many shared and supported Paul's mission. Many women are mentioned in positions of leadership. Some risked their lives for him. Many early Christian churches met in believers' homes. Many of these Christians were gracious in their care for Paul. He referred to some of them as apostles. Ordinarily this meant those authorized to be evangelists, transmitters of the Good News of Jesus the Christ.

[Romans 16:1-7]

- For most of Christianity's history, women have not been permitted to be official leaders. They were leaders, however, in early churches. Why has women serving in leadership roles in the Christian church been controversial?

Apostle also described those whom Jesus himself sent directly to broadcast the Good News. Paul closed his letter commending the obedience of the Roman Christians. He was full of joy over them. He wanted them to be wise about what was good and innocent about what was evil. Paul retained the services of Tertius as a scribe for this letter. Tertius himself stated that he wrote down this letter.

[Romans 16:8-24]

> Paul mentions women and men who risked their lives for him. What was the basis for such loyalty to this apostle?

Paul ended his letter to the Roman Christians with the following benediction: "Now to him who is able to establish you by my gospel and the proclamation of Jesus Christ, according to the revelation of the mystery hidden for long ages past, but now revealed and made known through the prophetic writings by command of the eternal God – so that all nations might believe and obey him – to the only wise God be glory forever through Jesus Christ! Amen."

[Romans 16:25-27]

> What was THE WAY of Jesus that Paul found?
>
> Have you found THE WAY of Jesus? If so, how has it changed your life?

FOR FURTHER DISCUSSION OR PERSONAL REFLECTION:

[ROMANS 15:17-19]
Paul lived by the power of the Spirit. We might think of this as living in the "God-Zone." In what ways do you see Paul living in the God-Zone?

What gave Paul the ever-renewing courage to stay on his course?

In what ways do you see yourself living in the God-Zone?

[ROMANS 15:14-21]
What change in the Church's approach to missions is needed to carry the gospel to places where it is "unknown"?

[ROMANS 16]
Early Christians often met in the homes of members. What benefits or problems do you see in members' homes being used for church meetings?

[ROMANS 16:25-27]
In his final benediction, Paul said the prophetic writings and proclamation of Jesus Christ point to the command of the eternal God that all nations might believe and obey him. What does this mean?

EPILOGUE

During the 12 sessions of this study, you've sampled a bit of what early Paul conveyed to believers in the early years of the church. By no means comprehensive, this study was intended to get you talking with others about the challenges faced by Christians throughout history and God's direction for his people in the new era of GRACE. Questions have guided your time of dialog during this study. We'd like to leave you with a few more questions to consider on your own.

1. Are you willing to ask Jesus to give you a new beginning with him and transform your life?

2. Can you make following him your highest priority?

3. What would you tell someone else about what you're learning about Jesus?

4. Are you willing to share the Good News about him with others in your world?

As you continue to journey with Jesus, please remember that you are not traveling alone. He's gone ahead of you to blaze the trail, and he promises to be with you every step of the way.

He promises to give a purposeful, flourishing and meaningful life now and for eternity to all who journey with him, to each person who affirms that Jesus is Lord and Savior. Moreover, he has promised to provide the wisdom, the power and even the words you need to invite others to follow him, too.

If you enjoyed this study of Paul's letter to the church in Rome, you may want to study the life of Jesus as told by the Apostle Mark. *YOUR INVITATION* is an 11-session small-group exploration designed to deepen your understanding of God's love and forgiveness as expressed in the life and teachings of Jesus Christ.

You may also want to consider studying the life of Jesus as told by the Apostle John. *TRANSFORMATION* is a 13-session small-group exploration designed to deepen your understanding of God's love and forgiveness as expressed in the life and teachings of Jesus Christ.

YOUR INVITATION and *TRANSFORMATION* from Living Dialog Ministries, are available from online retailers and bookstores everywhere.

Please visit our website, www.lifesbasicquestions.com, for a place to engage some of the core questions of life. The website is designed to be a user-friendly way to dialog about the kinds of issues you encountered in your study of Paul's letter to the Romans. There is also a place on the website for visitors to ask their own questions, and receive a confidential response from the Living Dialog Ministry team. It's a helpful, no-cost resource you can share with others.

ABOUT US
Directors of the Living Dialog Ministries

JOHN C. (JACK) DANNEMILLER, Chairman and CEO of The Living Dialog Ministries, is the former Chair and CEO of Applied Industrial Technologies, a Fortune 1000 corporation. He is a 30-year leader of small group Bible studies, a frequent speaker at Christian Businessmen events, and a lecturer at the Weatherhead Graduate School of Business of Case Western Reserve University where he was honored with the Distinguished Alumni Award.

IRVING R. STUBBS, President Emeritus of The Living Dialog Ministries, is a minister with degrees from Davidson College and Union Theological Seminary in New York. He served in pastorates, an urban ministry, and consultant to business, media, religious, government, and professional organizations and their executives in North America, Europe, and Asia. He is the author and co-author of books, articles, and learning resources.

HENRY R. (HARRY) POLLARD, IV, Secretary of The Living Dialog Ministries, is Chairman, Partner, and Practicing Attorney with Parker, Pollard, Wilton & Peaden, PC of Richmond, Virginia where he has practiced law for more than 40 years. He has served as an officer and director of numerous businesses including banking, real estate, and financial entities. He is co-founder and Chairman of The Values Institute of America.

KENT E. ENGELKE, Treasurer of The Living Dialog Ministries, is a Managing Director and Chief Economic Strategist for Capitol Securities Management, a $6.1 billion asset management company, and has served as a director of several publicly traded banks and mortgage banking firms. His views on the economy and the markets are routinely solicited by major media outlets. He credits God for the words he writes daily and thanks God for courage and perseverance in overcoming obstacles.

BRIAN N. REGRUT, Executive Director of The Living Dialog Ministries, is a former public relations executive and consultant, corporate speech writer, author and lecturer serving clients in the fields of telecommunications, financial services and education. He has served in a variety of church leadership roles including preaching and teaching. He and his wife of 51 years have taught Sunday School together and have led small group Bible studies for many years.

A THOUGHT-PROVOKING EVANGELISM TOOL FOR CHURCHES AND ORGANIZATIONS

For those on a journey of discovery, finally answers to the profound questions of life. This little book has been distributed to thousands.

Available in bulk at a reasonable cost with a customized cover featuring your logo and message from your church or organization.

Join the dialog
www.lifesbasicquestions.com

For pricing email
lifesbasicquestions@outlook.com

CHECK OUT OUR OTHER SMALL GROUP EXPLORATIONS

TRANSFORMATION

is designed to lead your small group through a rewarding study of the life Jesus as related by the Apostle John.

During the 13 sessions filled with thought-provoking questions, you will engage with others in an interactive format allowing you to gain new insights into Jesus, God's son and mankind's savior.

YOUR INVITATION

helps guide small groups in an exciting exploration, through Intentional dialog, of the Gospel of Mark.

Each of the 11 sessions starts with a thought-provoking question that leads the group into a short, biblically-accurate narrative interspersed with questions the

www.ingramcontent.com/pod-product-compliance
Lightning Source LLC
Chambersburg PA
CBHW072106290426
44110CB00014B/1853